The author would like to thank everyone who has helped with this book,
and with special thanks to Ernie and Mavis Davis; Nancy Mary Goodall;
M.D. How & Son, Chesham, Bucks; Caroline Lushington; Sue Miller;
Whitbread & Company PLC (Whitbread Hop Farm, Paddock Wood, Kent).

First American edition published 1989 by SIMON AND SCHUSTER BOOKS FOR YOUNG
READERS, Simon & Schuster Building, Rockefeller Center, 1230 Avenue of the
Americas, New York, New York 10020. Originated by J.M. Dent & Sons Ltd.
91 Clapham High Street, London SW4 7TA. First published in Great Britain in 1988.
Copyright © 1988 by Jane Miller. All rights reserved including the right of
reproduction in whole or in part in any form. Printed and bound by L.E.G.O.
Vicenza. SIMON AND SCHUSTER BOOKS FOR YOUNG READERS is a trademark of
Simon & Schuster Inc. 10 9 8 7 6 5 4 3 2 1

Library of Congress Cataloging-in-Publication Data

Miller, Jane, 1925-, Farm noises. Summary: Presents the distinctive sounds
made by two dozen animals, birds, and machines that may be heard on farms.
1. Farm sounds – Juvenile literature.   [1. Animal noises.   2. Bird song.
3. Farm sounds] I. Title. S519. M549 1989   636'.01   88-18540
ISBN 0-671-67450-1

For Edward

FARM NOISES

JANE MILLER

Simon and Schuster Books for Young Readers
Published by Simon & Schuster Inc., New York

Roosters crow:
cock-a-doodle-do

Hens cluck.
Chicks cheep

Donkeys bray:
ee-aw

Horses neigh
and snort

Sheep and lambs
baa

Crows call:
kaaah kaaah kaaah

Bees buzz-*z-z-z z-z-z*

Mice squeak: *ee-ee-ee*

Pigs grunt:
oink oink oink

Piglets squeal

Dogs bark and growl:
wuff-wuff, grrr-grrr
Puppies yap

Cats and kittens
meow and purr

Birds sing
and chirp

Frogs croak:
rib-it rib-it rib-it

Ducks and ducklings go
quack-quack

Streams gurgle

Bulls bellow

Cows moo

Combine harvesters roar

Tractors go
brum-brum

Geese honk.
Goslings cheep

Some owls hoot: *tu-wit tu-whoo*.
But barn owls shriek

Goats bleat:
maa-maa

And turkeys go
gobble-gobble